WORKBOOK FOR
UNDERSTANDING LANGUAGE STRUCTURE, INTERACTION, AND VARIATION, *SECOND EDITION*

An Introduction to Applied Linguistics and Sociolinguistics for Nonspecialists

Steven Brown
Salvatore Attardo
Cynthia Vigliotti

Youngstown State University

THE UNIVERSITY OF MICHIGAN PRESS

Copyright © by the University of Michigan 2005
All rights reserved
ISBN 0-472-03068-X
Published in the United States of America by
The University of Michigan Press
Manufactured in the United States of America
∞ Printed on acid-free paper

2008 2007 2006 2005   4 3 2 1

No part of this publication may be reproduced, stored in a retrieval system, or transmitted in any form or by any means, electronic, mechanical, or otherwise, without the written permission of the publisher.

Contents

Workbook for the Second Edition of

Understanding Language Structure, Interaction, and Variation

This workbook provides students with exercises to help in the study of linguistics. The workbook is aligned with the materials in *Understanding Language Structure, Interaction, and Variation,* Second Edition, but it is otherwise independent from it (i.e., students may do the exercises without referring to the book, provided, of course, they know the relevant material). Clearly, it would have been impossible to design exercises for all the chapters of the book and probably not even desirable. *Understanding Language Structure, Interaction, and Variation* already includes a few exercises/research projects in each chapter that can be used in classroom-based assignments should the instructor desire to assign them or should students want to deepen their understanding of a subject. The materials presented here focus primarily on those areas of **phonetics, morphology, syntax,** and **semantics** where students traditionally require more practice. Grammar and historical linguistics are also included. In keeping with the introductory nature of the coverage of *Understanding Language Structure, Interaction, and Variation,* no formal phonology or morphology problems are provided since they are meant for advanced students. The answer key for the workbook can be found online at *www.press.umich.edu/esl/tm/.* A key is not provided for all exercises.

These exercises are the result of several years' experience teaching introductory courses in linguistics for a variety of audiences and in a variety of settings. All three authors share responsibility for the materials herein, but in fairness, the majority of the exercises were designed by Cynthia Vigliotti.

We hope that both students and instructors will find these exercises useful. Any feedback, especially from those instructors/students who have new ideas for problems/exercises or from those who might require exercises in areas that we have not covered, would be greatly appreciated.

The authors would like to thank the following students who contributed in one way or another to the workbook: Sherry Bosley, Regina Donaldson, Julie Fieldhouse, Daniel Fuller, Andrea Harvey, and Rebecca Thorndike.

Cynthia L. Vigliotti, Salvatore Attardo, and Steven Brown
Youngstown, OH
2005

Practice for Chapter 2

The Building Blocks of Language

EXERCISES FOR 2.2.   THE SOUNDS OF LANGUAGE (PHONETICS)

The following 12 exercises will help the students practice their International Phonetic Alphabet (IPA) symbols, their transcription skills, and their skill at reading in IPA. By doing so, they will acquire valuable insights in the sound-to-spelling correspondences of English and will gain expertise in decoding IPA transcriptions of pronunciations.

Teachers may want to warn their students that often their pronunciation may vary significantly from that of the authors of the workbook and/or their classmates and teachers, and that this should not distress them. Caution should be exercised in using the key to the exercises, although some alternate pronunciations are provided. Teachers of non-native speakers of English should exercise particular caution in assigning these exercises.

Exercise 1.   Stress Placement

Provide a sentence for each pronunciation of the following words. Consult the dictionary if you need help distinguishing between them. (See textbook 2.2.1.)

1. compact: a. I bought a new com´pact for my makeup.

                b. This machine compacts´ the garbage.

2. ab´stract: _____

   abstract´:   _____

3. per´vert: _____

   pervert´:   _____

4. ad´dict: _____

   addict´:   _____

5. im´pact: _____

   impact´:   _____

6. con´vict: _____

   convict´:   _____

7. re´bel: _____

   rebel´:   _____

8. ob´ject: _____

   object´:   _____

9. ex´tract: _____

   extract´: _____

10. pres´ent: _____

   present´: _____

11. con´duct: _____

   conduct´: _____

12. per´fect: _____

   perfect´: _____

13. con´tent: _____

   content´: _____

14. mi´nute: _____

   minute´: _____

Exercise 2.   Natural Classes

A **natural** class is any group of sounds that share some phonetic feature. Therefore, all **stops** are a natural class; all **vowels** are another, as are all **voiceless stops,** all **nasals,** all **front vowels,** etc. In the following sets of sounds, identify the sound that does <u>not</u> belong to the natural class. Mark the odd sound, and identify the class to which the others belong. The first one has been done for you. (See textbook 2.2.1.)

1.
```
p
b
t
d
┌───┐
│ v │
└───┘
```

2.
```
ð
ʃ
f
θ
h
```

3.
```
w
m
p
b
f
```

4.
```
d
t
l
w
n
```

5.
```
e
i
o
ɔ
u
```

6.
```
g
v
z
ŋ
k
```

1. [v] does not belong; the others are stops

2. _____

3. _____

4. _____

5. _____

6. _____

Exercise 3.   Phoneme Identification

Identify the number of phonemes in each of the words in the following list. Then, write the word in the appropriately numbered box (the numbers indicate number of phonemes). Pay attention to the way the words *sound*, not the way they are spelled. Remember, **diphthongs count as one sound.** (See textbook 2.2.1.)

2	3	4	5
		align	

align	dough	laughs	sheep
axe	enough	law	sleigh
breaks	father	lay	sneeze
breath	faxed	leap	spleen
breathes	fields	neigh	teacher
breed	fourth	plough	thorough
bunnies	gnaw	rough	tow
cries	kissed	says	true
dew	knob	scares	woe
doe	know	singer	wreath

Exercise 4. *Phonetic Description of Consonants*

Provide the phonetic symbol and the full description for each underlined sound in each of the following words. (See textbook 2.2.1.)

	Symbol	*Place*	*Voicing*	*Manner*
o<u>p</u>en	[p]	bilabial	voiceless	stop
psy<u>ch</u>ology				
de<u>s</u>ire				
li<u>ng</u>er				
counte<u>d</u>				
<u>ph</u>one				
la<u>b</u>or				
recei<u>pt</u>				
a<u>g</u>itate				
crea<u>t</u>ure				
stro<u>ng</u>er				
<u>th</u>ere				
ce<u>m</u>ent				
trea<u>s</u>ure				
li<u>c</u>ense				
<u>th</u>in				
<u>gn</u>aw				
<u>wh</u>o				
in<u>v</u>ite				
ti<u>ss</u>ue				
butche<u>r</u>				
<u>l</u>eery				
q<u>u</u>een				
<u>y</u>ear				
wri<u>t</u>er				

Exercise 5. Phonetic Description of Vowels

Provide the phonetic symbol and the full description for each underlined vowel sound in each of the following words. (See textbook 2.2.1.)

   Note: For diphthongs, you must provide the articulation for both sounds.

	Symbol	Tip of Tongue	Body of Tongue	Tense/Lax	Example
r<u>ei</u>gn	[e]	front	mid	tense	date
C<u>ae</u>sar					
g<u>ue</u>st					
l<u>au</u>gh					
c<u>au</u>ght					
s<u>ew</u>er					
d<u>oi</u>ly					
v<u>i</u>sion					
<u>ai</u>sle					
cr<u>oo</u>ked					
c<u>o</u>vert					
b<u>o</u>ther					
b<u>ou</u>gh					

Exercise 6.   *Silent Letters*

I. Underline the silent letters in the following words. The first one has been done for you. (See textbook 2.2.1.)

mnemonic	gnaw	science
sword	pterodactyl	write
island	knot	debt
lamb	whole	role
corps	bough	night
resign	psychology	aisle

II. Now, phonetically transcribe the same words. The first one has been done for you. (See textbook 2.2.1.)

mnemonic	[nimɔnək]	whole	_____
sword	_____	bough	_____
island	_____	psychology	_____
lamb	_____	write	_____
corps	_____	science	_____
resign	_____	debt	_____
gnaw	_____	role	_____
pterodactyl	_____	night	_____
knot	_____	aisle	_____

Exercise 7.   Recognizing Consonant Sounds

Read the top word in each column, and note the sound underlined and in boldface type. Then, circle the words below it that also feature the same sound, not necessarily in the same position. To help you, the phonetic symbol is provided for that sound. (See textbook 2.2.1.)

con**t**ent	**k**ing	a**b**le	**s**erious	en**d**ure
[t]	[k]	[b]	[s]	[d]
kissed	knight	subtle	succeed	radiator
nestle	character	adaptable	cancel	patty
catch	success	thumb	decent	cad
butter	cease	debt	roses	ratify

forget	mi**m**ic	**r**eason	**w**inter	perha**p**s
[f]	[m]	[r]	[w]	[p]
tough	mnemonic	wrong	through	receipt
fall	lamp	fear	reward	raspberry
alpha	dumb	carp	prawn	psychic
laughter	omit	wrestle	wring	trap

thistle	**g**oing	**l**azy	no**n**sense	re**v**iew
[θ]	[g]	[l]	[n]	[v]
eighth	garden	tortilla	damn	of
the	gnome	talk	know	love
either	signal	call	corn	valiant
ether	magic	please	knee	marvel

cheer	**j**ump	**y**ellow	**z**ealous	**sh**ine
[tʃ]	[dʒ]	[y]	[z]	[ʃ]
machine	fudge	cynical	resign	action
rich	logical	mythology	example	martial
chorus	gelatin	canyon	raises	insurance
ache	page	gyrosphere	walks	childish

gara**ge**	wri**t**er	go**tt**en	**th**ere	**h**elp
[ʒ]	[ɾ]	[ʔ]	[ð]	[h]
confusion	ladle	attain	the	khaki
leisure	kitten	letter	rhythm	ash
pressure	water	uh-oh	sixth	wreath
rouge	actor	matter	another	historical

Exercise 8.   Recognizing Vowel Sounds

Read the top word in each column, and note the sound that is underlined and in boldface type. Then, circle the words below it that feature the same sound, not necessarily in the same position. To help you, the phonetic symbol is provided for that sound. (See textbook 2.2.1.)

weight	brief	math	time	debt
[e]	[i]	[æ]	[ay]	[ɛ]
grief	vie	lathe	deny	redo
height	friend	father	trim	sense
rain	grieve	author	tray	read
seize	dried	rather	science	delay

cop	pinch	donor	put	choice
[ɔ]	[ɪ]	[o]	[ʊ]	[oy]
taught	likely	though	lungs	violet
look	inspire	ton	rut	poignant
cope	thing	prone	push	trio
chalk	active	crow	crook	oil

pasta	loot	frown
[a]	[u]	[aw]
erase	book	raw
past	glue	rough
east	lose	thaw
father	attitude	trousers

Exercise 9.   Phonetic Transcription

Transcribe these words using the phonetic alphabet. Remember your glides and diphthongs!
The first one has been done for you. (See textbook 2.2.1.)

1. thousand	[θawzənd]	21. beings	_____
2. bathtub	_____	22. fusion	_____
3. trauma	_____	23. language	_____
4. pure	_____	24. emotional	_____
5. beauty	_____	25. eighth	_____
6. Wednesday	_____	26. statue	_____
7. larynx	_____	27. chair	_____
8. slyly	_____	28. fume	_____
9. action	_____	29. player	_____
10. isn't	_____	30. hours	_____
11. August	_____	31. plush	_____
12. vision	_____	32. chop	_____
13. radiator	_____	33. church	_____
14. sometimes	_____	34. down	_____
15. leisure	_____	35. fluff	_____
16. million	_____	36. cough	_____
17. sink	_____	37. beep	_____
18. total	_____	38. bit	_____
19. time	_____	39. heap	_____
20. raisin	_____	40. dew	_____

Exercise 10a.   Reverse Transcription

Transcribe the following phonetically spelled words into their English equivalents. The first one has been done for you. (See textbook 2.2.1.)

1. [plʌʃ] plush

2. [tʃɪp] _____

3. [pitʃ] _____

4. [brawn] _____

5. [rʌf] _____

6. [læf] _____

7. [krip] _____

8. [fɪt] _____

9. [tʃip] _____

10. [nuw] _____

11. [dɛt] _____

12. [kʌt] _____

13. [rot] _____

14. [kɔt] _____

15. [θri] _____

16. [flayt] _____

17. [kʊʃən] _____

18. [tʃʌrp] _____

19. [hʌrt] _____

20. [hæt] _____

Exercise 10b.   Reverse Transcription

Transcribe the following phonetically spelled words into their English equivalents. The first one has been done for you. (See textbook 2.2.1.)

1. [layiŋ]   _____lying_____

2. [bird]   _____

3. [dʒʌmp]   _____

4. [ʃɔl]   _____

5. [ayðər]   _____

6. [tʃayəld]   _____

7. [dʒʌdʒ]   _____

8. [tʃest]   _____

9. [kwayt]   _____

10. [nɔkʃəs]   _____

11. [iθər]   _____

12. [baw]   _____

13. [duw]   _____

14. [frut]   _____

15. [plen]   _____

16. [powtʃ]   _____

17. [θim]   _____

18. [ɔro]   _____

19. [leyiŋ]   _____

20. [εθəl]   _____

Exercise 10c.   *Reverse Transcription*

Transcribe the following phonetically spelled words into their English equivalents. The first one has been done for you. (See textbook 2.2.1.)

1. [kloð]   clothe   11. [sɪksθ]   _____

2. [rʌŋ]   _____   12. [əlayn]   _____

3. [hʌntəd]   _____   13. [spes]   _____

4. [tʃir]   _____   14. [fɪʃ]   _____

5. [tʃardʒ]   _____   15. [neʃən]   _____

6. [hɔntəd]   _____   16. [θisəs]   _____

7. [mɛɾəl]   _____   17. [pʊriŋ]   _____

8. [θif]   _____   18. [kerfəl] _____

9. [rɔŋ]   _____   19. [ʃʊd]   _____

10. [tʃendʒ] _____   20. [θiri]   _____

Exercise 10d.   Reverse Transcription

Transcribe the following phonetically spelled words into their English equivalents. The first one has been done for you. (See textbook 2.2.1.)

1. [tʃɔk]   _____chalk_____   11. [dʒɛləs]   _____

2. [əplay]   _____   12. [ʃules]   _____

3. [æpəl]   _____   13. [dʒulz]   _____

4. [myuzɪʃən]   _____   14. [trayfəl] _____

5. [kɔləm]   _____   15. [sɛkʃən]   _____

6. [rayɾər]   _____   16. [rɛkərd]   _____

7. [redar]   _____   17. [rəkord]   _____

8. [pælət]   _____   18. [riɾər]   _____

9. [iresər]   _____   19. [læɾərəl] _____

10. [awtredʒ]   _____   20. [dʌtʃ]   _____

Exercise 11.   Phrasal Reverse Transcription

The IPA transcriptions that follow are the names of popular musical groups/singers. Transcribe them into their English-spelled equivalents. The first one has been done for you. (See textbook 2.2.1.)

1. [ðə birəlz]

   _____the Beatles_____

2. [fɪʃ]

   _____

3. [dev mæθyuz bænd]

   _____

4. [blɔndi]

   _____

5. [ðə vaynz]

   _____

6. [wizər]

   _____

7. [rʌn di ɛm si]

   _____

8. [bisti boyz]

   _____

9. [ɛvənɛsənts]

   _____

10. [ðə dʒɛts]

    _____

11. [awtkæst]

    _____

12. [ɛmɪnəm]

    _____

13. [erosmɪθ]

    _____

14. [ðə tʃʌrtʃ]

    _____

15. [ðə pəlis]

    _____

16. [blɪŋk wʌnetituw]

    _____

17. [iŋkyubəs]

    _____

18. [æləs ɪn tʃeynz]

    _____

19. [dʒɔn meyər]

    _____

20. [mətælɪka]

    _____

21. [ðə rəmonz]

    _____

22. [daydo]

    _____

23. [pʌdəl ʌv mʌd]

    _____

24. [krid]

    _____

Exercise 12.   Transcription Errors

Correct the errors in the following phonetic transcriptions by underlining the incorrect sounds. Transcribe the words correctly in the spaces provided. There may be more than one error in each word. (See textbook 2.2.1.)

1. metal   [mɛd̲əl]   [mɛɾəl]

11. theory   [ðiri]   _____

2. error   [errər]   _____

12. language [læŋgwədʒ] _____

3. board   [borəd]   _____

13. police   [polis]   _____

4. cloth   [clɔð]   _____

14. sculpt   [skulpt]   _____

5. paint   [paynt]   _____

15. write   [wrɪt]   _____

6. magnet [magnɛt]   _____

16. grace   [grays]   _____

7. fact   [fakt]   _____

17. awful   [awfəl]   _____

8. length   [lɛnθ]   _____

18. easy   [eze]   _____

9. weight   [wayt]   _____

19. mortal [mɔrtəl]   _____

10. color   [kʌlor]   _____

20. chased [tʃaced]   _____

EXERCISES FOR 2.3.   WORDS AND THEIR PARTS (MORPHOLOGY)

Exercises 13–18 focus primarily on morphemic breakdown of words, word formation techniques, and identification of morphemes. They should be helpful for students who need to build their lexicon or who need practice in identifying word formation techniques.

Teachers may want to remind their students that comprehensive English dictionaries provide etymological information, which may be indispensable in answering some of the questions.

Exercise 13.   Free Morphemes

I. Underline the free morpheme (or root) in each of the following words. The first one has been done for you. (See textbook 2.3.2.)

mindful	fortunate	resourceful	quickly
adulthood	revisit	powerful	written
illegal	portable	undress	fulfilling
returnable	alignment	cleverly	substitution
spacious	penniless	poems	sculptor

II. Break down the following words by placing each morpheme into the appropriate column. The first one has been done for you. (See textbook 2.3.2.)

Word	Prefix/es	Root	Suffix/es
discredited	dis	credit	ed
interplanetary			
reservations			
illegibly			
factually			
biodegradable			
realignment			
unspoken			
personable			
overestimated			

Exercise 14. Morphemic Analysis

Break the following words into morphemes and then indicate the root morpheme. The first one has been done for you. (See textbook 2.3.2.)

1. un / impeach / abil / ity   root: _____ impeach _____

2. unpredictable   root: _____

3. indefensible   root: _____

4. inalienable   root: _____

5. representative   root: _____

6. undefeated   root: _____

7. destabilizing   root: _____

8. reprogramming   root: _____

9. uncomprehending   root: _____

10. unflappable   root: _____

11. reprioritize   root: _____

12. insurmountable   root: _____

13. involuntarily   root: _____

14. illegalizing   root: _____

15. unsurpassed   root: _____

16. nonconfrontational   root: _____

17. disrespectful   root: _____

18. unfashionable   root: _____

19. nonalcoholic   root: _____

20. infrequently   root: _____

Exercise 15.   Identify Roots with Affixes

In the passage, underline each root that has an affix attached to it. The first one has been done for you. (See textbook 2.3.3.)

Many **attempts** have been made by writers on art and poetry to define beauty in the abstract, to express it in the most general terms, to find some universal formula for it. The value of these attempts has most often been in the suggestive and penetrating things said by the way. Such discussions help us very little to enjoy what has been well done in art or poetry, to discriminate between what is more and what is less excellent in them, or to use words like *beauty, excellence, art, poetry,* with a more precise meaning than they would otherwise have. Beauty, like all other qualities presented to human experience, is relative; and the definition of it becomes unmeaning and useless in proportion to its abstractness. To define beauty, not in the most abstract but in the most concrete terms possible, to find not its universal formula, but the formula which expresses most adequately this or that special manifestation of it, is the aim of the true student of aesthetics.

Source: From Walter Pater, *The Renaissance: Studies in Art and Poetry.*

Exercise 16. *Identifying Inflectional Morphemes*

Underline all of the inflectional morphemes in this passage from *Gulliver's Travels* by Jonathan Swift. Be sure to include those irregular verbs and plurals that may be less obvious. Those in the first sentence have been done for you. (See textbook 2.3.4.)

Hav**ing** thus answer**ed** the only objection that can ever be rais**ed** against me as a traveller, I here take a final leave of all my courteous readers, and return to enjoy my own speculations in my little garden at Redriff; to apply those excellent lessons of virtue which I learned among the Houyhnhnms; to instruct the Yahoos of my own family, as far as I shall find them docible animals; to behold my figure often in a glass, and thus, if possible, habituate myself by time to tolerate the sight of a human creature; to lament the brutality to Houyhnhnms in my own country, but always treat their persons with respect, for the sake of my noble master, his family, his friends, and the whole Houyhnhnm race, whom these of ours have the honour to resemble in all their lineaments, however their intellectuals came to degenerate.

Exercise 17a.   Word Formation Techniques

Identify the word formation technique in each of these words. (See textbook 2.3.5.)

1. RSVP   _acronym_____

2. horseshoe   _____

3. gas   _____

4. ATM   _____

5. smog   _____

6. Velcro   _____

7. sitcom   _____

8. RAM   _____

9. FedEx   _____

10. gangster   _____

11. earring   _____

12. memo   _____

13. ASAP   _____

14. moped   _____

15. cheeseburger   _____

16. dorm   _____

17. notebook   _____

18. styrofoam   _____

19. fridge   _____

20. anklet   _____

21. band aid   _____

22. sushi   _____

23. washable   _____

24. flu   _____

25. rockumentary   _____

Exercise 17b. *Word Formation Techniques*

Identify the word formation technique(s) in each of these words. <u>Note:</u> More than one
technique may apply. (See textbook 2.3.5.)

1. childish   __derivation__

2. readability   _____

3. sunglasses   _____

4. photo   _____

5. breathalyzer _____

6. megabyte   _____

7. CPU   _____

8. Doc   _____

9. Kleenex   _____

10. spam   _____

11. feminist   _____

12. blacklist   _____

13. steno   _____

14. coffee   _____

15. to enthuse   _____

16. Fruitopia   _____

17. kickstand   _____

18. Xerox   _____

19. Reaganomics _____

20. scraper   _____

21. pancake   _____

22. to emote   _____

23. sidewalk   _____

24. headache   _____

25. scanner   _____

Exercise 17c.   Word Formation Techniques

Identify the word formation technique(s) in each of these words. <u>Note:</u> More than one technique may apply. (See textbook 2.3.5.)

1. math   _clipping_____

2. neighborhood _____

3. sailboat _____

4. USA _____

5. swimathon _____

6. DOS _____

7. racetrack _____

8. phys. ed. _____

9. football _____

10. CD _____

11. suitcase _____

12. resurrect _____

13. spork _____

14. milkshake _____

15. to page _____

16. to televise _____

17. fairground _____

18. exam _____

19. UFO _____

20. Jello _____

21. skateboard _____

22. demo _____

23. radar _____

24. transceiver _____

25. preempt _____

Exercise 18.　Reverse Word Formation Techniques

List three examples for each word formation technique featured. The first examples have been done for you for items 1–3. (See textbook 2.3.5.)

1. derivation

adulthood

_____

_____

2. compounding

pocketbook

_____

_____

3. clipping

fridge

_____

_____

4. blending

_____

_____

_____

5. backformation

_____

_____

_____

6. invention

_____

_____

_____

7. borrowing

_____

_____

_____

8. acronyms

_____

_____

_____

9. calque

_____

_____

_____

Exercise 19.   Idioms

Define the literal and idiomatic meaning of the following expressions. Instructors may also ask students to include—on separate pieces of paper—examples of other idioms that mean the same thing (e.g., *buy the farm* also means *to die*). (See textbook 2.3.6.)

Expression	Literal	Idiomatic
Kick the bucket	Hit the bucket with a foot	die
A dime a dozen		
At first blush		
Be in the hole		
Bring home the bacon		
Clam up		
Cook the books		
Cost an arm and a leg		
Cry over spilt milk		
Foot the bill		
Gravy train		
Let sleeping dogs lie		
Make ends meet		
Nest egg		
Out to lunch		
Piece of cake		
Shoot the breeze		
Split hairs		
Suck up to someone		
Take something with a grain of salt		
The shit hit the fan		
To ask for trouble		
To be a big cheese		
To be all ears		
To be all thumbs		
To be the apple of someone's eyes		
What you see is what you get		

EXERCISES FOR 2.4.   THE WAY SENTENCES ARE PUT TOGETHER/ 2.5. TYPES OF SENTENCES (SYNTAX)

Many of these exercises revolve around tree diagramming. The purpose of this skill is to be able to visualize (and hence better understand) the structure of sentences. To this end, it is important to be neat when doing tree diagrams. Students (and many others) find this difficult and often frustrating. The best way to draw clear, useful tree diagrams is to draw a draft tree and, after having established the structure of the sentence, plan out the final tree, so as to be able to leave enough space for the various constituents of the sentence. Needless to say, practice makes perfect.

To this purpose, we present a few hundred sentences, divided by difficulty level: **simpler kernel sentences** are followed by five groups of sentences in which one (and only one) transformation has applied. Sentences containing **subordinate clauses and coordinated constituents** follow. Finally, there is a section of 200 hundred mixed sentences in which **transformations, subordinations, and coordinations may or may not appear, either singly or in combination.** We recommend that students undertake the diagramming of only kernel sentences at first. Transformations and other more complex structures can be introduced at a later time. More advanced students may of course be asked to diagram transformed sentences. Teachers may also find it useful to assign homework using this progression. The mixed sentences may be assigned to students even if not all the structures used have been introduced, provided that the teacher simplify the sentences as required (or indicate to the students which sentences they can diagram). The "answers" to the tree diagramming are not provided in the answer key.

Exercise 20.   Identifying Constituents

In this passage, determine whether each bolded part of the text is a constituent (C) or not (N). (See textbook 2.4.2.)

To the present generation _____, that is to say, **the people a few** _____ years on **the hither** _____ and thither side of thirty, the **name of Charles** ____ Darwin stands **alongside of those of Isaac Newton and Michael Faraday** _____; and, like them, calls up **the grand ideal** _____ of a searcher after **truth and interpreter** _____ of Nature. They think of **him who bore it** _____ as a rare combination of **genius, industry, and unswerving veracity**_____, who earned his place **among the most** _____ famous men of **the age** _____ by sheer native power, in the teeth **of a gale of popular prejudice** _____, and **uncheered by a sign** _____ of favour or appreciation from the official fountains of honour; as **one who in spite of an acute sensitiveness to praise and blame** _____, and notwithstanding provocations which might have excused any outbreak, kept himself **clear of all envy** _____, hatred, and malice, nor **dealt otherwise than fairly and justly** ____ with the unfairness and injustice **which was showered upon him** _____; while, to **the end of his days** _____, he was **ready to listen with patience and respect** _____ to the most insignificant of **reasonable objectors** _____.

Source: From Thomas Henry Huxley, "On the Reception of the *Origin of Species.*"

Exercise 21. Immediate Constituency

Identify and place in brackets the NP (noun phrase) and VP (verb phrase) in each of these sentences. The first one has been done for you. (See textbook 2.4.2.)

                NP   VP

1. [The umbrella] [is in the hall closet with the coats].

2. Jane loves black raspberry ice cream.

3. My neighbor walks with his beagle in the park.

4. The wheel has been used for thousands of years.

5. Goodyear discovered the process of vulcanization.

6. The young woman combing her hair in the window waved to us.

7. Linguistics is a required course for most majors in English.

8. Our little sister plays soccer for her elementary school team.

9. We found several boxes of old LPs in the basement of the new house on Elm Street.

10. The gentleman with the top hat visits the woman on the second floor.

Exercise 22.   *Sentence Diagramming without Transformations*

These sentences are kernel sentences. On separate pieces of paper, draw a tree diagram for each. (See textbook 2.4.2.)

1. The boy went to the store for the groceries.
2. My mother loves leek soup with croutons.
3. The beer from the new keg tastes a bit weird.
4. The players in the band practiced the new songs for weeks on end.
5. His nephew lost the keys to his house after the wild party on Saturday.
6. The CEO of the company fired all the employees after the failed IPO.
7. I lost my shirt in the stock market after the recession.
8. The cute little girl rode her bike in the park under the trees.
9. The musicians performed the piece with great gusto for a full house.
10. The accordion player bowed to her audience with a big smile on her face.
11. The theater season began with a performance of a play by Beckett.
12. The monkey on the branch threw a banana at the mouse under the table.
13. The boyfriend of the linguist sat in the back of the room at the conference.
14. The artist finished her piece in time for the opening of the show.
15. The philosopher meditated on the meaning of life for many years.
16. The customer in the checkout line asked for plastic bags for his groceries.
17. The pool player pondered the difficult shot for several minutes during the tournament.
18. The ungrateful child neglected his ailing parents for many years.
19. Untrustworthy politicians lie during electoral campaigns for personal gain.
20. The woman in the red dress danced all night with many different partners.
21. The architect prepared the plans for the new building of the university.
22. The proofreader found many mistakes in the article by the careless journalist.
23. The teenagers shopped at the mall for many hours every day throughout the summer.
24. The girl with the ponytail skated with her friends at the rink for two hours on Sunday.
25. The shadow of night descended on the valley after sunset.
26. Many English majors go to law school after graduation from a B.A. program.
27. Pilates lengthens the muscles through a series of stretching exercises.
28. The grocer stocks five varieties of apples from a local farm.
29. The child with the red lollipop in his hand cries about his allergy shot every week.
30. The French poodle with the woman in the pink Lagerfeld suit is the newest addition to the House of Chanel.

Exercise 23a.   Transformations

These sentences have undergone syntactic transformations. Identify which transformation has been applied based on the options in the chart. The first one has been done for you. (See textbook 2.4.2.)

Passive	P
Question	Q
Negation	N
Particle hop	H
Dative movement	D

1. Our parents were surprised by the anniversary party.   ___P___

2. Jane picked the prescription up for her elderly uncle.   _____

3. Did you ask John about the concert on Tuesday?   _____

4. We will drop your dry cleaning off after school.   _____

5. Are we going to the store on the way to your meeting?   _____

6. The clerk gave us the discount on the television.   _____

7. Tom didn't buy the CD for his sister in North Carolina.   _____

8. The song was remade by the jazz group on its new CD.   _____

9. Sue was disappointed by her grade on the final.   _____

10. We sent our mother flowers for her birthday.   _____

Exercise 23b.   Transformations

Remove the transformation from each sentence, and rewrite the kernel sentence. The first one has been done for you. (See textbook 2.4.2.)

1. Our parents were surprised by the anniversary party.

   The anniversary party surprised our parents.

2. Jane picked the prescription up for her elderly uncle.

   _____

3. Did you ask John about the concert on Tuesday?

   _____

4. We will drop your dry cleaning off after school.

   _____

5. Are we going to the store on the way to your meeting?

   _____

6. The clerk gave us the discount on the television.

   _____

7. Tom didn't buy the CD for his sister in North Carolina.

   _____

8. The song was remade by the jazz group on its new CD.

   _____

9. Sue was disappointed by her grade on the final.

   _____

10. We sent our mother flowers for her birthday.

    _____

Exercise 24. PSG Grammars

Write the simplest PSG (phrase structure grammar) that can generate the following sentences.

Note: We are asking for the simplest PSG since obviously the PSG grammar presented in the textbook 2.4.2 is capable of generating all the kernel sentences of English. The first one has been done for you.

1. The boy likes apples.

   NP → (Art) + N
   VP → V + NP
   Art → the
   N → boy, apples
   V → likes

2. Mary went to the store with her friends.

3. The boys from Brazil arrived at the airport.

4. The man in a grey suit ate pizza for dinner.

5. Children eat Pop Tarts for breakfast.

6. The colorful tent covered the members of the wedding party.

7. A boy by the name of John led the school anthem.

8. I am an Englishman in New York.

9. The general liked the smell of napalm in the morning.

10. The name of the new baby is a secret.

Exercise 25. Identifying Passives

In this passage from a famous text in English literature, all the verbs appear in boldfaced print. Underline those that are passives. (See textbook 2.5.)

I **have been assured** by a very **knowing** American of my acquaintance in London, that a young healthy child well **nursed**, is, at a yearold, a most delicious **nourishing** and wholesome food, whether **stewed**, **roasted**, **baked**, or **boiled**; and I make no doubt that it **will** equally **serve** in a fricasie, or a ragout.

I **do** therefore humbly **offer** it to publick consideration, that of the hundred and twenty thousand children, already **computed**, twenty thousand **may be reserved** for breed, whereof only one fourth part **to be** males; which is more than we **allow** to sheep, black cattle, or swine, and my reason **is**, that these children **are** seldom the fruits of marriage, a circumstance not much **regarded** by our savages, therefore, one male **will be sufficient to serve** four females. That the **remaining** hundred thousand **may**, at a year old, **be offered** in sale to the persons of quality and fortune, through the kingdom, always **advising** the mother **to let them suck** plentifully in the last month, so as **to render** them plump, and fat for a good table. A child **will make** two dishes at an entertainment for friends, and when the family **dines** alone, the fore or hind quarter **will make** a reasonable dish, and **seasoned** with a little pepper or salt, **will be** very good **boiled** on the fourth day, especially in winter.

Source: From Jonathan Swift, "A Modest Proposal for preventing the children of poor people in Ireland, from being a burden on their parents or country, and for making them beneficial to the publick" (1729).

Exercise 26a.   Active vs. Passive Sentences

Identify the following sentences as featuring either the **active** (A) or the **passive** voice (P). The first one has been done for you. (See textbook 2.5.)

1. The bookshelf was built by a master woodworker. **P**

2. Our aunt is arriving by plane tomorrow morning. _____

3. The sofa was moved before the walls were painted. _____

4. The actor was excited by her new role in the action film. _____

5. The painting on the wall is by Mary Cassatt. _____

6. The criminal was brought before a grand jury. _____

7. My favorite song is by System of a Down. _____

8. The bill was drafted by a senator from Montana. _____

9. The child was playing by the parked cars. _____

10. Timothy Leary was an influential writer during the 1960s. _____

11. We went to a play by Edward Albee on our visit to New York. _____

12. The stack of books for the garage sale is by the door. _____

13. I saw the latest film by the Coen brothers last weekend. _____

14. The CEO was brought up on charges of fraud by the prosecutors. _____

15. The professor was trained by the nation's leading linguists at MIT. _____

Exercise 26b.   Active vs. Passive Sentences

Convert the sentences that are passive into the active voice. (Some may already be in the active voice.) The first one has been done for you. (See textbook 2.5.)

1. The bookshelf was built by a master woodworker.

   A master woodworker built the bookshelf.

2. Our aunt is arriving by plane tomorrow morning.

   _____

3. The sofa was moved by the tenants before the walls were painted.

   _____

4. The actor was excited by her new role in the action film.

   _____

5. The painting on the wall is by Mary Cassatt.

   _____

6. The criminal was brought before a grand jury.

   _____

7. My favorite song is by System of a Down.

   _____

8. The bill was drafted by a senator from Montana.

   _____

9. The child was playing by the parked cars.

   _____

10. Timothy Leary was an influential writer during the 1960s.

   _____

11. We went to a play by Edward Albee on our visit to New York.

_____

12. The stack of books for the garage sale is by the door.

_____

13. I saw the latest film by the Coen brothers last weekend.

_____

14. The CEO was brought up on charges of fraud by the prosecutors.

_____

15. The professor was trained by the nation's leading linguists at MIT.

_____

Exercise 27. Sentence Diagramming, Passive Transformations

These sentences have all had the passive transformation (see textbook 2.5) applied to the kernel sentence. Remove the transformation, and on separate sheets of paper, diagram the kernel sentences.

1. Mary was surprised by his passionate embrace.
2. The new computer was attacked by a virus after a week.
3. The president of the company was fired by the board of directors.
4. The capitalist mode of production is strengthened by periodical outbreaks of violence.
5. The best bicycles are built by artisans in small workshops in Northern Italy.
6. Mona was kissed by all the people at the party for her graduation.
7. No one was surprised by the news of his early retirement.
8. The procedures are evaluated by the government in secret hearings.
9. Children are delighted by the presents for their birthdays.
10. Santa was surprised by the fire in the chimney of the house.
11. The thieves were discovered by a clever detective after a lengthy investigation.
12. Cynthia is preoccupied by the payments for her new car.
13. The judge was convinced by the evidence in the case against the corporate officers.
14. My philosophical beliefs are influenced by neo-positivism.
15. The hopes of the skater were dashed by the verdict of the judges.
16. The paintings were hung on the walls of the museum by the curator.
17. Many fingerprints were left by the burglars in this unusual case.
18. The onlookers were dismayed by the late arrival of the artists.
19. The diners were confused by the many options on the menu of the restaurant.
20. The envelope was mailed by someone in Florida.
21. The manifesto was written by the Ph.D. student on an old typewriter at the cabin in Montana.
22. The Doors' song was remade by George Thorogood.
23. Our windows were broken by an explosion at the fireworks factory near our home.
24. Mistakes were made by the Reagan administration.
25. The shoes were designed by Tom Ford for his last collection at Gucci.

Exercise 28.   Sentence Diagramming, Question Transformations

These sentences have all had the question transformation (see textbook 2.5) applied to the kernel sentence. Remove the transformation, and on separate sheets of paper, diagram the kernel sentence.

1. Is Mary in the house with her friends?
2. Did the police arrest the bank robbers?
3. Were his colleagues happy for the winner of the lottery?
4. Do bears walk in the woods?
5. Was the decision to attend college difficult?
6. Did your rich aunt build a house in the suburbs for her children?
7. Did the pizza arrive on time for the Super Bowl party?
8. Did your friend lose a lot of weight during the first week of his diet?
9. Did the people at the picnic like the homemade potato salad with chives?
10. Was your sister happy about the gifts from your trip to Europe?
11. Did Nancy like the selection of flowers at the nursery?
12. Are all the people in that van with the band?
13. Were the questions on the exam from the first three chapters of the book?
14. Did you get the coupon for a free dinner at the new restaurant in yesterday's paper?
15. Am I the first applicant for the position of editor at the newspaper?
16. Did you put the cans of vegetables in the pantry?
17. Did the olive tree in the garden survive throughout the winter?
18. Was Bob surprised by the divorce papers from his wife?
19. Did the professor treat her students to pizza at the end of the semester?
20. Were you in the store for the fitting of the bridesmaids' gowns?
21. Is the new anchor on *60 Minutes* from the *CBS Evening News*?
22. Do you remember the words to your alma mater?
23. Can we agree on the color for the living room walls?
24. Are there many first-time performers on Karaoke Night?
25. Am I the youngest student in the graduate seminar on X-bar theory?

Exercise 29.   Sentence Diagramming, Particle Hopping Transformations

These sentences have all had the particle hopping transformation (see textbook 2.5) applied to the kernel sentence. Remove the transformation, and on separate sheets of paper, diagram the kernel sentence.

1. Ann stood Jim up after their second date.
2. John took Mary out to an expensive restaurant for her birthday.
3. The lion tamer put the clowns up for the night.
4. The soldiers of the battalion put the camp up before nightfall.
5. Kim firmed her decision up before the day of graduation.
6. Bob squandered his political capital away on a campaign against his opponent.
7. The girl with the pearl earring sat the jar up on the table.
8. The father wrapped his child up in a cozy blanket.
9. The lawyer for the government finished the case up with a compelling argument.
10. The judge handed the sentence down to the accused parties.
11. Sam made many interesting stories up for the children in her library group.
12. Jack looked the reference up in the first book from his reading list.
13. The union let the workers down in their first meeting with the administration.
14. Sarah called Tim up for the party at Trevor's house.
15. Rapunzel let her hair down on the side of the castle for the prince.
16. Ben put the shades down after the gunshot in the backyard of his house.
17. The parents sent the child out of the room for a few minutes during the discussion.
18. Frank put the martinis away with gusto until his collapse into a drunken stupor.
19. Jill called her girlfriends up for a trip to the lake last weekend.
20. Steve told Sal off about the late delivery of the manuscript for the book.
21. The administration wound the meeting up for the holiday weekend.
22. The chef at the four-star hotel skims the fat off of the boiling sauce.
23. The old tomcat coughed the hairball up on the new rug after several minutes.
24. The MacArthur Foundation picks the brightest scholars out of many candidates.
25. We sent the children off to camp for the entire summer.

Practice for Chapter 3

How Do We Mean Things?

EXERCISES FOR 3.1.   THE MEANING OF WORDS (SEMANTICS)

These exercises focus primarily on **constituent analysis** (an area of semantics that is seldom practiced first hand by students) and on **pragmatics.** They should help students master the often difficult differences between implicatures, presupposition, and speech acts.

Teachers may want to warn their students about avoiding *what if* situations (along the lines of *but what if one is in a coma, but the brain is still alive . . .*). In general, if a situation has to be described explicitly, then it should not be used; in other words, presuppositions, implicatures, etc., are based on "normal" stereotypical situations, not on exceptional ones.

Exercise 30. Denotative and Connotative Meaning

For each of the following words, list the denotative or literal meaning and then any connotations you may have for that word. (Connotations will vary.) The first one has been done for you. (See textbook 3.1.3.)

1. *bachelor*

   Denotation: _____ unmarried adult male human being _____

   Connotations: _____ carefree, eligible, messy, desirable lifestyle _____

2. *chick* (human female)

   Denotation: _____

   Connotations: _____

3. *dot-com*

   Denotation: _____

   Connotations: _____

4. *dude*

   Denotation: _____

   Connotations: _____

5. *European*

   Denotation: _____

   Connotations: _____

6. *fashionable*

   Denotation: _____

   Connotations: _____

7. *gossip*

Denotation: _____

Connotations: _____

8. *librarian*

Denotation: _____

Connotations: _____

9. *organic*

Denotation: _____

Connotations: _____

10. *perpetrator*

Denotation: _____

Connotations: _____

11. *pre-owned*

Denotation: _____

Connotations: _____

12. *rag* (newspaper with half-sized pages)

Denotation: _____

Connotations: _____

13. *rhinoplasty*

Denotation: _____

Connotations: _____

14. *schnozzle*

   Denotation: _____

   Connotations: _____

15. *scientific*

   Denotation: _____

   Connotations: _____

16. *spinster*

   Denotation: _____

   Connotations: _____

17. *Third World*

   Denotation: _____

   Connotations: _____

18. *trendy*

   Denotation: _____

   Connotations: _____

Exercise 31.   Semantic Features: Seating Furniture

Do a feature semantics analysis of the following nouns related to the semantic field of furniture. You may need to do some research to find out exactly what the objects are, and you may need to use more than six features. In that case, add more columns or add the features in the space below.

Chair	[+ with back]					
Couch						
Love seat						
Armchair						
Bench						
Ottoman						
Recliner						
Carver chair						
Club chair						
Bean bag chair						
Stool	[- with back]					

You will need to review section 3.1.1 of the textbook.

Exercise 32.   Semantic Features: Cocktails

Do a feature semantics analysis of the following nouns related to the semantic field of cocktails. You may need to do some research to find out exactly what the beverages include (not necessarily at your local bar), and you may need to use more than six features. In that case, add more columns or add the features in the space below.

Martini	[+ vermouth]					
Cosmopolitan						
Gin and Tonic						
Long Island Iced Tea						
Screwdriver						
Manhattan						
Bellini						
Bloody Mary						
Cuba Libre						
Margarita						
Mint Julep						
Mimosa						
White Russian						

 You will need to review section 3.1.1 of the textbook.

Exercise 33.   Semantic Features: Cooking Verbs

Do a feature semantics analysis of the following verbs related to the semantic field of cooking. You may need to do some research to find out exactly what each cooking technique involves, and you may need to use more than six features. In that case, add more columns or add the features in the space below.

(Pan) Fry	[+ in fat]					
Deep fry	[+ in fat]					
Braize	[- in fat]					
Grill						
Poach						
Roast						
Flambé						
Toast						
Sear						
Sauté						
Broil						
Boil						
Steam						
Bake						
Barbeque						

 You will need to review section 3.1.1 of the textbook.

Exercise 34. *Semantic Features: Kinship Terms*

Do a feature semantics analysis of the following nouns related to the semantic field of kinship terms (family relations). You may need to do some research to find out exactly what the terms describe, and you may need to use more than six features. In that case, add more columns or add the features in the space below.

mother	[+ parent of self]	[+ female]				
father		[- female]				
sister						
brother						
daughter	[- parent of self]					
son						
daughter-in-law						
son-in-law						
uncle						
aunt						
cousin						
nice						
nephew						
grand-father						
grand-mother						
great grand father						
great grand mother						
godfather						
godmother						

You will need to review section 3.1.1 of the textbook.

Exercise 35.   Semantic Features: Pasta Semantics

Do a feature semantics analysis of the following semantic field of pasta shapes. You may need to do some research in the pasta aisle of your grocery store or online to find out what the pasta shapes are. You may need to use more than six features. In that case, add more columns or add the features in the space below.

Spaghetti	[+ long]					
Vermicelli	[+ long]					
Fettuccine	[+ long]					
Ditalini	[- long]					
Orzo						
Rotini						
Fusilli						
Penne						
Pennette						
Lasagne						
Rigatoni						
Mostaccioli						
Trenette						
Cannelloni						

You will need to review section 3.1.1 of the textbook.

Exercise 36. Deictic Expressions

In these passages, underline each deictic expression (see textbook 3.2.1) you can identify. In the spaces provided below each line, identify what they refer to.

I suddenly became conscious that someone was looking at me. I turned halfway round, and

saw Dorian Gray for the first time. When our eyes met, I felt that I was growing pale. A curious

sensation of terror came over me. I knew that I had come face to face with someone whose mere

personality was so fascinating that, if I allowed it to do so, it would absorb my whole nature, my

whole soul, my very art itself.

Dorian, from the moment I met you, your personality had the most extraordinary influence over

me. I was dominated, soul, brain, and power by you. You became to me the visible incarnation

of that unseen ideal whose memory haunts us artists like an exquisite dream. I worshipped you

. . . I hardly understood it myself. I only knew that I had seen perfection face to face.

Source: From Oscar Wilde, *The Picture of Dorian Gray.*

Exercise 37.   Indirect Speech Acts

Indicate the illocutionary force of the following speech acts. Explain why they are *indirect* speech acts. The first one has been done for you.

1. Can you pass the salt?

   __Pass the salt._____

2. May I help you? (said by a security guard)

   _____

3. Do you know "Feelings"? (said to a pianist)

   _____

4 . Excuse me? (said to someone who has offended you)

   _____

5. Would you mind stepping out of the way?

   _____

6. Does my smoking bother you?

   _____

7. Are you sure you don't want more cake?

   _____

8 Well, I have to get up very early. (said to lingering guests)

   _____

9. Will there be anything else? (said by a server after a meal is cleared)

   _____

10. That's an interesting idea (said after a not-so-smart comment)

    _____

Exercises 38.   Implicatures

Which maxims of the Cooperative Principle does each starred sentence violate in each little vignette? Note that a sentence may violate more than one maxim. The first one is done for you. (See textbook 3.2.3.)

Describe the implicatures generated by the violation and the inferential path to reach them.

> Reporters interviewing a spokesperson for the government.
>
> *Reporter:* "What is the administration going to do about this problem?"
> **Spokesperson:* "I can assure you that we are considering all available options and that we will respond in a manner that is both appropriate and efficacious."
>
> answer: manner, quantity, relevance (statements are obvious), and possibly quality

1. Mary and Susan are talking.

   Mary: "Yesterday, I went out with this guy who has all these sexy friends . . ."
   Susan: "And you didn't ask me to come along?"
   Mary: "It didn't occur to me."
   *Susan: "Nice friend you are."

2. *Father to his daughter in her messy room:*

   * "Perhaps you could condescend to performing some cleaning up-type activities, at your earliest convenience."

3. Mario is a good cook. His friend Gertrude is constantly pestering him to teach her how to cook. Mario agrees to show her his famous spaghetti recipe.

   Mario: "So you take a big pot, fill it with water, put it on the stove, turn on the burner, wait until the water boils. . ."

4. John and Bob are talking at a party about Frank's recent break up. As they talk, Frank walks up to them, but John cannot see him.

   John: ". . . and I think that Frank made a big mistake."
   Bob: "I just bought a really nice coat at Banana Republic."

5. Mary is considering buying a new car. The salesperson at the car dealership is showing her an SUV.

   Mary: "What kind of mileage does it get?"
   Salesperson: "Have you noticed the upholstery?"

6. Mary and Bob are having a business meeting with the CEO of their hi-tech company. Mary has just presented a proposal for a project that will save the company large amounts of money.

   Mary: ". . . and therefore I think we should go with my proposal."
   Bob: "How would you know? Women don't understand technology."

Exercise 39.   Presuppositions

Identify the presuppositions in these sentences. The first one has been done for you. (See textbook 3.2.3.)

1. The game is played in Cleveland.
    There exists a game and Cleveland.
    A game may be played (e.g., the game is scheduled).

2. Our team wins the championship.

3. Mary buys a bottle of water.

4. Bob goes to school in Indiana.

5. Bill is no longer single.

6. Todd is late for class every Friday.

7. Don's computer broke down.

8. Stu is dead.

Historical Linguistics

These exercises focus on etymology. Students should be warned that most likely they will need to use a full-sized dictionary to answer the questions.

Exercise 40.   Etymological Matching

Each word in the left-hand column is related etymologically to one in the right-hand column. Identify the match, and draw a line connecting the two. Next, using an etymological dictionary, explain how the two words are related, as in the example in which *estimate* is borrowed from Latin, *esteem* is borrowed from French, and the French word was itself derived from the Latin root, *aestimare*. Write the explanation on the line to the right of the right-column word of each pair you connect.

Left	Right	Explanation
cataclysm	feat	_____
estimate	ghost	_____
fact	skirt	_____
faction	poignant	_____
gentile	advice	_____
guest	fashion	_____
hospital	treason	_____
legal	clyster	_____
minion	matrix	_____
mother	witty	_____
pedagogy	esteem	Latin *aestimare* : French *estime*
pungent	loyal	_____
redemption	gentle	_____
shirt	mania	_____
tradition	pedophile	_____
video	poison	_____
wisdom	ransom	_____

Exercise 41a.   Which Word Does Not Fit?

In the following rows of three words, only two of the words are related etymologically. Circle the word that does not belong. You will probably need to use a dictionary. The first one has been done for you.

	park	paddock	pork
1.	chair	cart	chariot
2.	manure	maneuver	manicure
3.	depot	deport	deposit
4.	fake	forge	fabric
5.	aim	maim	esteem
6.	bend	bond	band
7.	respect	repose	respite
8.	phlegm	flame	flimsy
9.	reason	ration	raisin
10.	fungus	sponge	expunge
11.	fiasco	flask	flash
12.	world	word	verb
13.	slime	salt	saliva
14.	quiet	coy	quite
15.	prayer	prize	praise
16.	pauper	poor	boor
17.	costume	custom	cushion
18.	cell	call	hall
19.	parabola	parole	pardon
20.	locust	lobster	lobe

Exercise 41b.   Which Word Does Not Fit?

In the following rows of three words, only two of the words are related etymologically. Circle the word that does not belong. You will probably need to use a dictionary.

1.	crate	barrel	hurdle
2.	furnish	veneer	venereal
3.	acute	cute	accuse
4.	jay	gay	game
5.	sinecure	secure	sure
6.	employ	impeach	implicate
7.	brother	friar	father
8.	listen	lurk	lark
9.	tuba	tulip	turban
10.	ticket	etiquette	picket
11.	pattern	patron	patchwork
12.	barge	cargo	charge
13.	restrain	restrict	retain
14.	faculty	fecundity	facility
15.	glamour	glitter	grammar
16.	quiet	quit	quilt
17.	lass	lace	lasso
18.	pope	papa	people
19.	robber	rogue	rover
20.	itch	inch	ounce

Exercise 41c.   Which Word Does Not Fit?

In the following rows of three words, only two of the words are related etymologically. Circle the word that does not belong. You will probably need to use a dictionary.

1.	dignity	dainty	deity
2.	parson	parsley	person
3.	surge	sergeant	servant
4.	keg	cave	cage
5.	cavalry	Calvary	chivalry
6.	udder	utter	outer
7.	supervisor	surveyor	surprise
8.	daft	deft	defy
9.	captain	chieftain	sergeant
10.	dauphin	orphan	dolphin
11.	cater	cattle	capital
12.	veer	whirl	warble
13.	vast	vest	waste
14.	temper	triumph	trump
15.	associate	assimilate	assemble
16.	zero	number	cipher
17.	belly	belfry	bellows
18.	beaker	pitcher	bottle
19.	credence	cadence	chance
20.	deplete	defect	defeat

Exercise 41d.   Which Word Does Not Fit?

In the following rows of three words, only two of the words are related etymologically. Circle the word that does not belong. You will probably need to use a dictionary.

1.	beak	bark	barge
2.	canal	channel	tunnel
3.	tamper	timbre	temper
4.	flower	flour	floss
5.	steak	steer	stock
6.	beam	boom	broom
7.	callus	calumny	challenge
8.	scandal	scurrilous	slander
9.	adamant	diamond	Adam
10.	two	devil	deuce
11.	place	plan	plaza
12.	stop	block	plug
13.	purge	scourge	excoriate
14.	raid	road	rage
15.	disc	discord	dish
16.	stack	stake	stick
17.	sovereign	subject	soprano
18.	attach	attack	attract
19.	musket	muskrat	mosquito
20.	participle	particle	parcel
21.	onion	bunion	union
22.	deck	thatch	thick
23.	aggravated	aggrieve	agriculture
24.	minion	dominion	danger

Practice for Chapter 19

English Grammar

These exercises will allow students to practice some of the grammatical points covered in a basic introduction to English grammar.

Teachers may want to use some of these exercises prior to teaching syntax, especially if tree diagramming will be used intensely.

Exercise 42a.   Basic Parts of Speech

Note the words in boldface in the passage. Using the abbreviations from the chart at the bottom of the page, label the words according to their part of speech. <u>Note:</u> If two words in a row are boldfaced, it is assumed that they are one part of speech only. (See textbook 19.1.)

As Gregor Samsa **awoke** _____ from unsettling dreams one **morning** _____, he found

himself _____ transformed **in** _____ his bed into a **monstrous** _____ vermin. He lay on

his hard armorlike **back** _____ and when he raised **his** _____ head a little he **saw** _____ his

vaulted _____ brown belly divided into sections **by** _____ stiff **arches** _____ from whose

height _____ the coverlet had **already** _____ slipped and was about **to slide** _____ off

completely. His many legs, which **were** _____ pathetically thin compared **to** _____ the **rest**

_____ of his bulk, flickered helplessly **before** _____ his eyes.

Noun	N
Verb	V
Auxiliary	AUX
Adjective	ADJ
Adverb	ADV
Article	ART
Preposition	P
Pronoun	PRO
Conjunction	C

Source: From Franz Kafka, *The Metamorphosis*, trans. Donna Freed.

Exercise 42b.   Basic Parts of Speech

Note the words in boldface in the passage. Using the abbreviations from the chart at the bottom of the page, label the words with the appropriate part of speech. If two words in a row are boldfaced, it is assumed that they are one part of speech only. (See textbook 19.1.)

A **spectre** _____ is **haunting** _____ Europe—**the** _____ spectre of Communism. **All** _____ the Powers of **old** _____ Europe **have** _____ entered **into** _____ a holy alliance **to** exorcise _____ this spectre: Pope and Czar, Metternich and Guizot, **French** _____ Radicals **and** _____ German police-spies.

Where _____ is the party in **opposition** _____ that has not been decried as Communistic by its opponents in power? Where the Opposition that has **not** _____ hurled **back** _____ the branding reproach **of** _____ Communism, against the **more** _____ advanced opposition parties, as well as against **its** _____ reactionary **adversaries** _____ ?

The **modern** _____ bourgeois society **that** _____ has sprouted from the ruins of feudal society **has** _____ not done away with **class** _____ antagonisms. It has but established **new** _____ classes, new conditions of oppression, new **forms** _____ of struggle in place of the old **ones** _____. Our epoch, the epoch of the bourgeoisie, possesses, **however** _____, this distinctive feature: it **has simplified** _____ the class antagonisms. Society as a whole is more **and** _____ more splitting up **into** _____ two great hostile camps, into two great classes, **directly** _____ facing each other: Bourgeoisie and Proletariat.

Noun	N
Verb	V
Auxiliary	AUX
Adjective	ADJ
Adverb	ADV
Article	ART
Preposition	P
Pronoun	PRO
Conjunction	C

Source: From Karl Marx and Friedrich Engels, *Manifesto of the Communist Party.*

Exercise 43.   Identifying Articles

In the passage, all articles have been removed. The places where an article stood are marked by the symbol [_____]. Your job is to insert the appropriate article within the brackets. The first one has been done for you. (See textbook 19.1.)

Radiation levels in [the] fenced, ground zero area are low. On [_____] average, [_____] levels are only 10 times greater than [_____] region's natural background radiation. [_____] one hour visit to [_____] inner fenced area will result in [_____] whole body exposure of one-half to one milliroentgen.

To put this in perspective, [_____] U.S. adult receives [_____] average exposure of 90 milliroentgens every year from natural and medical sources. For instance, [_____] Department of Energy says we receive between 35 and 50 milliroentgens every year from [_____] sun and from 20 to 35 milliroentgens every year from our food. Living in [_____] brick house adds 50 milliroentgens of exposure every year compared to living in [_____] frame house. Finally, flying coast to coast in [_____] jet airliner gives [_____] exposure of between three and five milliroentgens on each trip.

Although radiation levels are low, some feel any extra exposure should be avoided. The decision is yours. It should be noted that small children and pregnant women are potentially more at risk than [_____] rest of [_____] population and are generally considered groups who should only receive exposure in conjunction with medical diagnosis and treatment. Again, [_____] choice is yours.

Source: From White Sand Missile Range, "Trinity Size, A National Historic Landmark."

Exercise 44.   Verb Constituency

In the passage, predicate units have been bracketed. Within each predicate unit, identify each verb unit as either a main verb (M) or an auxiliary verb (A). Note that the treatment of subordinate clauses is not consistent (i.e., in some cases, subordinate clauses are marked as a separate predication and in others, they are not—do not attach any significance to this fact). The first one has been done for you. (See textbook 19.2.1.)

(M)

In the second century of the Christian Æra, the empire of Rome [**comprehended the fairest part of the earth, and the most civilized portion of mankind**]. The frontiers of that extensive monarchy [**were guarded by ancient renown and disciplined valor**]. The gentle but powerful influence of laws and manners [**had gradually cemented the union of the provinces**]. Their peaceful inhabitants [**enjoyed and abused the advantages of wealth and luxury**]. The image of a free constitution [**was preserved with decent reverence**]: the Roman senate [**appeared to possess the sovereign authority, and devolved on the emperors all the executive powers of government**]. During a happy period of more than fourscore years, the public administration [**was conducted by the virtue and abilities of Nerva, Trajan, Hadrian, and the two Antonines**]. It [**is the design of this, and of the two succeeding chapters, to describe the prosperous condition of their empire**]; and afterwards, from the death of Marcus Antoninus, [**to deduce the most important circumstances of its decline and fall**]; a revolution which [**will ever be remembered and is still felt by the nations of the earth**].

The principal conquests of the Romans [**were achieved under the republic**]; and the emperors, for the most part, [**were satisfied with preserving those dominions which had been acquired by the policy of the senate, the active emulations of the consuls, and the martial enthusiasm of the people**]. The seven first centuries [**were filled with a rapid succession of triumphs**]; but it [**was reserved for Augustus to relinquish the ambitious design of subduing the whole earth, and to introduce a spirit of moderation into the public councils]. Inclined to peace by his temper and situation, it [was easy for him to discover that Rome, in her present exalted situation, had much less to hope than to fear from the chance of arms]; and that, in the prosecution of remote wars, the undertaking [became every day more difficult, the event more doubtful, and the possessions more precarious, and less beneficial]. The experience of Augustus [added weight to these salutary reflections], and effectually [convinced him that, by the prudent vigor of his counsels, it would be easy to secure every concession] which the safety or the dignity of Rome [might require from the most formidable barbarians]. Instead of exposing his person and his legions to the arrows of the Parthians, he [obtained by an honorable treaty, the restitution of the standards and prisoners] which [had been taken in the defeat of Crassus].

Source: From Edward Gibbon, Esq., *History of the Decline and Fall of the Roman Empire.*

Exercise 45.   Identifying Tensed/Untensed Verbs

All verbs in the passage appear in boldfaced print. Underline the untensed verbs. Notice how the participle of the first verb, which is a passive, is untensed and therefore underlined. The first one has been done for you. (See textbook 19.2.1.)

It **is** a truth universally **<u>acknowledged</u>**, that a single man in possession of a good fortune, **must be** in **want** of a wife.

However little **known** the feelings or views of such a man **may be** on his first entering a neighbourhood, this truth **is** so well **fixed** in the minds of the surrounding families, that he **is considered** the rightful property of some one or other of their daughters.

"My dear Mr. Bennet," **said** his lady to him one day, "have you **heard** that Netherfield Park **is let** at last?"

Mr. Bennet **replied** that he **had** not.

"But it **is**," **returned** she; "for Mrs. Long **has** just **been** here, and she **told** me all about it."

Mr. Bennet **made** no answer.

"**Do** you not **want to know** who **has taken** it?" **cried** his wife impatiently.

"YOU **want to tell** me, and I **have** no objection **to hearing** it."

This **was** invitation enough.

"Why, my dear, you **must know**, Mrs. Long **says** that Netherfield **is taken** by a young man of large fortune from the north of England; that he **came** down on Monday in a chaise and four **to see** the place, and **was** so much **delighted** with it, that he **agreed** with Mr. Morris immediately; that he **is to take** possession before Michaelmas, and some of his servants **are to be** in the house by the end of next week."

Source: From Jane Austen, *Pride and Prejudice.*

Exercise 46a.   Identifying Nouns

All the nouns in the passage appear in boldfaced print. In the parentheses that follow each, identify the nouns as Count (C) or Mass (M), Proper (P) or Common (CO), and Abstract (A) or Concrete (CT). The first one has been done for you. (See textbook 19.3.)

To the thinking **man** (*C, CO, CT*) there are few **things** (_____) more disturbing than the **realization** (_____) that we are becoming a **nation** (_____) of minor **poets** (_____). In the good old **days** (_____) **poets** (_____) were for the most part confined to **garrets** (_____), which they left only for the purpose of being ejected from the **offices** (_____) of **magazines** (_____) and **papers** (_____) to which they attempted to sell their **wares** (_____). Nobody ever thought of reading a **book** (_____) of **poems** (_____) unless accompanied by a guarantee from the **publisher** (_____) that the **author** (_____) had been dead at least a **hundred** (_____) **years**. **Poetry** (_____), like **wine** (_____), certain **brands** (_____) of **cheese** (_____), and public **buildings** (_____), was rightly considered to improve with **age** (_____); and no **connoisseur** (_____) could have dreamed of filling himself with raw, indigestible **verse** (_____), warm from the **maker** (_____).

Today, however, **editors** (_____) are paying real **money** (_____) for **poetry** (_____); **publishers** (_____) are making a **profit** (_____) on **books** (_____) of **verse** (_____); and many a young **man** (_____) who, had he been born earlier, would have sustained **life** (_____) on a **crust** (_____) of **bread** (_____), is now sending for the **manager** (_____) to find out how the **restaurant** (_____) dares try to sell a **fellow** (_____) **champagne** (_____) like this as genuine **Pommery** (_____) Brut. Naturally this is having a marked **effect** (_____) on the **life** (_____) of the **community** (_____). Our **children** (_____) grow to **adolescence** (_____) with the **feeling** (_____) that they can become **poets** (_____) instead of working. Many an **embryo** (_____) **bill** (_____) **clerk** (_____) has been ruined by the heady **knowledge** (_____) that **poems** (_____) are paid for at the **rate** (_____) of a **dollar** (_____) a **line** (_____). All over the **country** (_____) promising young **plasterers** (_____) and rising young **motormen** (_____) are throwing up steady **jobs** (_____) in order to devote themselves to the new **profession** (_____). On a sunny **afternoon** (_____) down in **Washington Square** (_____) one's **progress** (_____) is positively impeded by the **swarms** (_____) of young **poets** (_____) brought out by the warm **weather** (_____).

Source: From P. G. Wodehouse, *The Alarming Spread of Poetry.*

Exercise 46b.   Identifying Nouns

All the nouns in the passage appear in boldfaced print. In the parentheses that follow each, identify the nouns as Count (C) or Mass (M), Proper (P) or Common (CO), and Abstract (A) or Concrete (CT). The first one has been done for you. (See textbook 19.3.)

In one of those beautiful **valleys** (*C, CO, CT*), through which the **Thames** (_____) (not yet pol-luted by the **tide** (_____), the scouring of **cities** (_____), or even the minor defilement of the sandy **streams** (_____) or **Surrey** (_____)) rolls a clear **flood** (_____ through flowery **meadows** (_____), under the shade of old **beech** (_____) **woods** (_____), and the smooth mossy **greensward** (_____) of the chalk **hills** (_____) (which pour into it their tributary **rivulets** (_____), as pure and pellucid as the **fountain** (_____) of **Bandusium** (_____), or the **wells** (_____) of **Scamander** (_____), by which the **wives** (_____) and **daughters** (_____) of the **Trojans** (_____) washed their splendid **garments** (_____) in the **days** (_____) of **peace** (_____), before the coming of the **Greeks** (_____)); in one of those beautiful **valleys** (_____), on a bold round-surfaced **lawn** (_____), spotted with **juniper** (_____), that opened itself in the bosom of an old **wood** (_____), which rose with a steep, but not precipitous **ascent** (_____), from the river to the **summit** (_____) of this **hill** (_____), stood the castellated **villa** (_____) of a retired **citizen** (_____). Ebenezer Mac **Crotchet** (_____), **Esquire** (_____), was the **London** (_____)-born **offspring** (_____) of a worthy **native** (_____) of the "north **countrie** (_____)," who had walked up to **London** (_____) on a commercial **adventure** (_____), with all his surplus **capital** (_____), not very neatly tied up in a not very clean **handkerchief** (_____), suspended over his **shoulder** (_____) from the **end** (_____) of a hooked **stick** (_____), extracted from the first **hedge** (_____) on his **pilgrimage** (_____); and who, after having worked himself a step or two up the **ladder** (_____) of **life** (_____), had won the virgin **heart** (_____) of the only **daughter** (_____) of a highly respectable **merchant** (_____) of **Duke's Place** (_____), with whom he inherited the honest **fruits** (_____) of a long series of ingenuous **dealings** (_____).

Source: From Thomas Love Peacock, *Crotchet Castle.*

Exercise 47a.   *Identifying Types of Determiners*

In the passage, all determiners have been underlined. In the spaces provided after each, identify them as *pre-* (PR), *post-* (PO), *central determinative* (CD), or *central indeterminative* (CI) determiners. The first one has been done for you. (See textbook 19.4.3.)

From <u>The</u> (__CD__) *Adventures of Pinocchio* by C. Collodi (transl. from <u>the</u> (_____) Italian by Carol Della Chiesa).

Chapter 1: How it happened that Mastro Cherry, carpenter, found <u>a</u> (_____) piece of wood that wept and laughed like <u>a</u> (_____) child

Centuries ago there lived—"<u>A</u> (_____) king!" my little readers will say immediately.

No, children, you are mistaken. Once upon <u>a</u> (_____) time there was <u>a</u> (_____) piece of wood. It was not <u>an</u> (_____) expensive piece of wood. Far from it. Just <u>a</u> (_____) common block of firewood, one of those thick, solid logs that are put on <u>the</u> (_____) fire in winter to make cold rooms cozy and warm.

I do not know how this really happened, yet <u>the</u> (_____) fact remains that one fine day <u>this</u> (_____) piece of wood found itself in <u>the</u> (_____) shop of <u>an</u> (_____) old carpenter. His real name was Mastro Antonio, but everyone called him Mastro Cherry, for <u>the</u> (_____) tip of his nose was so round and red and shiny that it looked like <u>a</u> (_____) ripe cherry.

As soon as he saw <u>that</u> (_____) piece of wood, Mastro Cherry was filled with joy. Rubbing his hands together happily, he mumbled half to himself: "This has come in <u>the</u> (_____) nick of time. I shall use it to make <u>the</u> (_____) leg of <u>a</u> (_____) table."

He grasped the hatchet quickly to peel off <u>the</u> (_____) bark and shape <u>the</u> (_____) wood. But as he was about to give it <u>the</u> (_____) <u>first</u> (_____) blow, he stood still with arm uplifted, for he had heard <u>a</u> (_____) wee, little voice say in <u>a</u> (_____) beseeching tone: "Please be careful! Do not hit me so hard!"

Exercise 47b.   Identifying Types of Determiners

In the passage, all determiners have been underlined. In the spaces provided after each, identify them as *pre-* (PR), *post-* (PO), *central determinative* (CD), or *central indeterminative* (CI) determiners. The first one has been done for you. (See textbook 19.4.3.)

To explain in what has consisted the revenue of the great body of the (**CD**) people, or what has been the (_____) nature of those funds, which, in different ages and nations, have supplied their annual consumption, is the (_____) object of these (_____) four first (_____) books. The (_____) fifth (_____) and last (_____) book treats of the (_____) revenue of the (_____) sovereign, or commonwealth. In this (_____) book I have endeavoured to shew, first, what are the (_____) necessary expenses of the (_____) sovereign, or commonwealth; which of those expenses ought to be defrayed by the (_____) general contribution of the (_____) whole society, and which of them, by that of some (_____) particular part only, or of some (_____) particular members of it: secondly, what are the (_____) different methods in which the (_____) whole (_____) society may be made to contribute towards defraying the expenses incumbent on the (_____) whole (_____) society, and what are the (_____) principle advantages and inconveniences of each of those (_____) methods; and, thirdly and lastly, what are the (_____) reasons and causes which have induced almost all (_____) modern governments to mortgage some part of this (_____) revenue, or to contract debts; and what have been the (_____) effects of those (_____) debts upon the (_____) real wealth, the (_____) annual produce of the land and labour of the (_____) society.

Source: From Adam Smith, *An Inquiry Into the Nature and Causes of the Wealth of Nations.*

Exercise 48.   Identifying Adjectives

In the passage, adjectives appear in boldfaced print. Indicate in the parentheses that follow each adjective whether the adjective is attributive (A) or predicative (P). The first one has been done for you. (See textbook 19.4.)

The **old** (___A___) stage coach was rumbling along the **dusty** (_____) road that runs from Maplewood to Riverboro. The day was as **warm** (_____) as midsummer, though it was only the middle of May, and Mr. Jeremiah Cobb was favoring the horses as much as possible, yet never losing sight of the fact that he carried the mail. The hills were **many** (_____), and the reins lay loosely in his hands as he lolled back in his seat and extended one foot and leg luxuriously over the dashboard. His brimmed hat of **worn** (_____) felt was well pulled over his eyes, and he revolved a quid of tobacco in his left cheek.

There was one passenger in the coach,—a **small** (_____) **dark** (_____) -haired person in a **glossy** (_____) **buff** (_____) calico dress. She was so **slender** (_____) and so stiffly **starched** (_____) that she slid from space to space on the leather cushions, though she braced herself against the middle seat with her feet and extended her cotton-gloved hands on each side, in order to maintain some sort of balance. Whenever the wheels sank farther than usual into a rut, or jolted suddenly over a stone, she bounded involuntarily into the air, came down again, pushed back her funny little straw hat, and picked up or settled more firmly a **small** (_____) **pink** (_____) sun shade, which seemed to be her chief responsibility,—unless we except a bead purse, into which she looked whenever the condition of the roads would permit, finding **great** (_____) **apparent** (_____) satisfaction in that its **precious** (_____) contents neither disappeared nor grew less. Mr. Cobb guessed nothing of these harassing details of travel, his business being to carry people to their destinations, not necessarily, to make them **comfortable** (_____) on the way. Indeed he had forgotten the very existence of this one **unnoteworthy** (_____) **little** (_____) passenger.

Source: From Kate Douglas Wiggin, *Rebecca of Sunnybrook Farm.*

Exercise 49.   Coordination and Subordination

Underline the coordinate or subordinate clause, and circle the conjunction in each sentence. In the space provided, identify the clause as either coordinate or subordinate. The first one has been done for you. (See textbook 19.6.1.)

1. Jane closed the office (when) the students finished their papers. ___subordination___

2. Steve is afraid that he bought the wrong book. _____

3. John left, and Mike went to the grocery store. _____

4. Mary drove through the night because her friends were tired. _____

5. Phone calls are expensive when the charges are reversed. _____

6. I contacted the store, and they held the suit for me. _____

7. We regret that we bought a television before the sale. _____

8. Jack drove through the stop sign and the officer cited him. _____

9. Sam ran across the street, while Jane waved from the door. _____

10. We will go to dinner after we visit your brother. _____

Exercise 50.   Restrictive vs. Non-Restrictive Relative Clauses

In the sentences, relative clauses are italicized. Identify them as restrictive (R) or non-restrictive (N). Normal punctuation has been removed to avoid nullifying the exercise (see textbook 19.6.1). Replace those commas that set aside non-restrictive clauses.

1. Mary's twin sister *who loves to gamble* lost a lot of money in the slots.   _____

2. Molly's sister *who just got married* had a fender bender while driving home.   _____

3. The student *you admitted to* the program won the soccer game.   _____

4. Any student *who gets straights As* should apply for scholarships.   _____

5. A student *who comes from abroad* may be disoriented by campus life.   _____

6. A student *whom I had forgotten* wrote me a letter thanking me for helping her.   _____

7. I remember Ann *whom you have met* from the art show.   _____

8. Bob's first book *which he wrote in two weeks* sold extremely well.   _____

9. The book *the teacher assigned* is hard.   _____

10. John believes that the coach *who led the team to the playoffs* is great.   _____

11. The pope *who was born in Poland* is very old.   _____

12. The president of the university *who likes fine dining* held a fund raiser.   _____

13. The girl *who is wearing a red dress* is my neighbor's daughter.   _____

14. The parents of the girl *who was arrested* had to post her bail.   _____

15. The man *who arrived late at the gate* missed the plane.   _____

Work Space for Transformations